This Side of Early

poems by
Naomi Ayala

Curbstone Press

Cover Artwork and Design: Virginia Robles-Villalba
Printed on acid-free paper by Bookmobile

Some of the poems in this manuscript have previously appeared in
*Ploughshares, Poetry Daily, Gargoyle, Saheb Ghalam Daily, Tiger
Tail, The Wind Shifts: New Latino Poetry, Seeds of Fire: Poetry from
the Other USA*, and *Poetic Voices Without Borders 2.*

This book was made possible by a grant from the DC Commission on
the Arts and Humanities.

 This book was published with the support of the
Connecticut Commission on Culture and Tourism
and donations from many individuals. We are very
Connecticut Commission   grateful for this support.
on Culture & Tourism

Library of Congress Cataloging-in-Publication Data

Ayala, Naomi, 1964-
 This side of early / by Naomi Ayala. -- 1st ed.
   p. cm.
 ISBN 978-1-931896-46-7 (pbk. : alk. paper)
 I. Title.

PS3551.Y23T47 2008
811'.54--dc22

                        2008045464

CURBSTONE PRESS   321 Jackson Street   Willimantic, CT 06226
       phone: 860-423-5110   e-mail: info@curbstone.org
                    www.curbstone.org

CONTENTS

v

囧 Perfection

ACKNOWLEDGEMENTS

My deepest thanks to Ariana Quiñones-Miranda, E. Ethelbert Miller, and Robert Russell for their ardent support and for aligning me with the type of work and resources that made it possible for me to have the time to write.

An artist's fellowship from the DC Commission on the Arts and Humanities was indispensable in beginning and developing the work included here. My thanks to its remarkable and humble staff.

I'm particularly grateful to Virginia Robles-Villalba, Ernesto Torres Almodóvar, Janette Smith, Henry Barbot, Gillian Cook, Andrew Lee, as well as Juliet Briscoe and the staff of the Adams Morgan Animal Clinic for their kindness, the caliber of their professional expertise, and their dedication to providing it to people of modest means.

Jason Shinder, Ed Ochester, Timothy Liu, and Amy Gerstler were unfailing in their encouragement and support, and extended correspondences that renewed my love of the writing life and my dedication to reading.

Liam Rector's love of and absolute belief in the autodidact and in a bold, rigorous, border-crossing education made it possible for me to achieve my longest held dream of earning a formal degree. May his tribe increase.

I am equally grateful to my loving family—the best a poet could have—my partner Robert Farr, who contributed greatly to final revisions, and my beautiful *comadres* and *compadres*:

Francisco Stork; Marge Plasmier; Bob and Cecilia Berner; Claire and Nick Zoghb; Stephen Kobasa; Richard Fewell; Martin Obeng; Juan Pérez; Darry Strickland; Jack Agüeros; Deborah Menkart, Marco Esparza, and Diego Esparza; Martín Espada; Joelle Maya Aubry; Carole Juarez; Sami Miranda; José Domínguez; Hiram Puig-Lugo; Sandy Taylor and Judith Doyle; Jantje Tielken; Bob Smith; Carlos Parada and *Para eso la palabra*; Rosina Talamantes; and Celeste Gúzman-Mendoza.

Since the publication of this book, three remarkable men—Sandy Taylor, Liam Rector, and Jason Shinder—have gone on to become teachers and luminaries elsewhere. May the gifts they've brought the world bring comfort to their families and beloveds.

for Marge,
who walks with me.

℔ You in the Me of I

Of those so close beside me, which are you?
God bless the Ground! I will walk softly there,
and learn by going where I have to go.

Theodore Roethke, "The Waking"

HOLE

One morning
they dig up the sidewalk and leave.
No sign of the truck,
only the large,
dark shadow digging and digging,
piling up sludge with a hand shovel
beside the only tree.
Two o'clock I come by
and he's slumbering in the grass beside rat holes.
Three and he's stretched across a jagged stonewall,
folded hands tucked beneath one ear—
a beautiful young boy smiling,
not the heavy, large shadow who can't breathe.
Four-thirty and the August heat
takes one down here.
He's pulled up an elbow joint
some three feet round.
At seven I head home for the night,
pass the fresh gravel mound,
a soft footprint near the manhole
like the "x" *abuelo* would place beside his name
all the years he couldn't write.

Every Throat

A *coquí* choir grades
the song of hedge grass.
Dark water laps at the bank.
This way,
where *tabaqueras* once
carried lanterns
to fields of spent hands,
cancered mouths and throats.
The way of the river
is clear eyes and fishing poles.
The old man, *abuelo*
draws bait from a bucket.
I claw the ground for earthworms.
A black, slick water-
slitherer, our first catch.
The dark sky seals my mouth.
The bent back man
does not fear Satan.
The word of God
breathes in every throat.
You can eat it, he says,
like butterfish we have for breakfast
with day-old bread
and ripe plantain,
bitter coffee to remember
how we wear this skin that hurts.

CUTTER

In the tool shed shack, plywood door
held open with the weight of a till,
he filed the edge down

on the electric sharpener he'd built himself.
Sparks he'd warned me about
grazed my face and arms
when he was not looking.

Sometimes we'd stay,
he on his little bench and I
a few feet away on the front stoop,
till the sun sank into the river
and it was time for roots and cod.

Once, my mother and father came to stay,
a night that I, under my *mosquitero*, looked out
for the creatures who watch you
when you're not looking.

And it was while most of those in the house slept
that a small bird of the night swooped down,
knocking into the wooden walls
and exposed beams of the house—
my mother screaming as if on fire.

Scrambling to free its legs
from her hair—rolled in a *dubi-du*
this night—the creature shrieked
while mami leapt and ran, calling for *abuelo*

who took his machete down
from the nails on a wall
and chased after her.
In the light of an oil lamp I watched
the glint of *abuelo*'s blade,

my mother beg with fear.

Between the running, head shaking
and screaming, the creature loosened itself
from the wrapped mane only
to meet the fate of sugarcane.

Proud he could still swing
that cutter of cane and *maleza*, *abuelo* carried
the winged corpse, still on the blade,
while I pleaded with him to let me keep it.

The bat was not
much bigger than my own hand—
its membrane wings like the leaves of an oak.
I studied the furry gash,
unfettered, and circled bone—
that day that death was first,
small and quick like my body.

IRONING

It took some convincing
for her to let me do it
but it was 25 cents a piece—
extra for pants,
nobody liked to do pants.

After clothes for a family
of seven, one a baby—baby
shouldn't wear wrinkled
clothes—I could iron
for those who brought
their bundles late afternoons
after school, and on weekends.

I was happy to coast
the heavy steamless iron
across the white
cotton of Social Fridays, the festivities
of spiritists, along gabardine
shop uniforms,
to spray water and starch
watching sunlight stream
through the windows—
back when I liked ironing.

The job didn't last long.
I was slacking off
on household chores,
mami said, just to make money.

I was happy doing almost
anything then, anything slow and quiet,
except for afternoon sweeping.
I was always fighting the wind.

Cada vez que los nombro
resucitan mis muertos.

Claribel Alegría, *Sorrow*

CADA VEZ
for Graciela

You pull sardines from a can,
fry them to eat with Wilfredo.
I pluck beads from a change purse
as if Tati were here.
As if these were her hands,
make white rice and fried eggs
for Baba because Baba made these.
We sit with the dead
in your kitchen, in mine.
You say *They are here.*
I don't turn to look.
You are a young girl
who laughs with Wilfredo now.
I run home to Baba,
convince Tati one day
I will be big and strong, carry her
in my arms to the ocean
where she will heal to walk again.
The dead remember us.
We gather in kitchens here,
sign our days with their names.

A Man Buys a Box of Cupcakes

Near the register he looks and digs
in secret pocket,
pulls at yellowed bills
drenched with sweat,

pays in full as the muttering
line eyes the hold up.

Above the Leukemia jug
his hands flutter to the mad
order of the unkempt,

stop to feel for another bill—
folded into tiny parts, like a poem
or despair—and

muttering something about hope,
he slips it in. The eyes of the children,
he turns and says to us, so close,
like ghosts of the night street.

In Adams Morgan, Two Years of Neighborhood-Wide Reconstruction Come to a Halt for the Night

And now, where the moon
rose behind here,
three stories loom—
inexplicable to the eye.
Floodlights lift
the puddles in the alley
to sad perfection.
No other brightness
to make beautiful
the edges of the dark.
Progress comes—
mocking visitor, a snoop—
to awed spaces
where we hold up
our pots and pans,
brush sweat
from our brows, wipe hands
on threadbare dishrags,
scold and kiss our children.
We should be glad—
some people tell us—
life is precious, move on.
Others say poverty
is redemption: leave.
And waiting to wake
we stir all night. We pray.
Our father, god
of the cupboard and the ladle,
redeem us.

BARRO

Red sun branding
the lap of love.
Cagüana, squatting over hot
stones to yield
to my birth of sky.
I fling my hot
breath to the world—
blessing and storm
—feeding my *maíz*
soul along the banks
of my people's song.
I am the river
and the women
who wash in it.
I am wind and *hurakán*,
scent of blood in the fields.
I was born a slow dance
of cane and bamboo—
knocking, always knocking.
Fertile or not,
I take up arms now.
The earth is a woman
who knows bow and arrow.

You in The Me of I

i.

I put out my hands.

I go to my drum.
My drum go to me.
To me my drum go.
Go drum to me.
Go drum.

*

When I'm scraping the pots,
I sing my own dance.
And when singing comes to me,

I lay my world with color—
round on my fingers,
a river, and let go.

*

I make love in my sleep.
Coyotes howl, put out all sound.
They get in my love.
They love in my sleep.

I love it like this.
Love breathes in my dreams.
In my love I sleep and in my love
no sleep sounds.

ii.

Where is my name,
this name, when I wake?

It burrows in the sheets,
all skin—
inside the morning,
breathes.

*

You are in my morning too.
Your breath hard,
then folding slowly
over the world.

*

This you in me wakes
and is always waking.
In the shape of a snowflake,
inside the mating of birds,
it falls into song.
In song we are made real,
we breathe.

Know singing before words.
Know goatskin.
Know the drum of the tree.

*

Into skin we are made,
all of my people.
Light of the moon on our backs.

Wind.

*

I have hallowed my sleep
like a gourd—this poor
instrument—with a
me in the me of an I.

iii.

Sad branches on the tree
outside the window,
bones catching snow.

I live in a branch of the tree,
in the cold I want to be safe from.
And in the cold, I love.

      *

So much simpler my I
rooted like a tree—
half earth, half sky.

      *

Of two worlds,
coming and going—
but I no full crow-woman yet.
Yet no full
crow-woman, crow.

      *

I go to my drum.
My drum go to me.
To me my drum go.

Go drum to me.
Go drum.

Dawn here.
Dawn.
Snow.

COCKROACH

I want to be able to feed on soap, paper, feces.

I want to live in a cardboard box,
eat the walls around me when I'm hungry.

I want a family of 12, 24, 48,
to nibble on feet and antennae,
bite into thoraxes,
when the food supply in my neighborhood runs out.

I want to avoid all light, live
to scavenge the darkness of houses,
scurry along walls and taste the waxy
spots of grease left behind.

I want the sweat of sink
pipes, a highway of bathtub drains.

I don't want to be polite.
I want to eat everything and survive it all.

JESUS COMES TO MT. PLEASANT IN SEARCH
OF SANZEN

Two drunks stumble in their best jeans in the valley of delight,
call out the *koans* of salvation.
Rutty color of oak bark along the dogwood street.
Brilliantined hair and front-stoop stubble.
Today Jesus walks among them, long locks
kissing the ground like points in a hem.
He lays in the street, calls from the doorways of winter.
Steam from the grillwork beside him, mere steam.
And he turns, turns in the republic of full-swing hips,
where two drunks in their best jeans
lift their hats and wave of the rain.

FOR YOU

Meet me where the barn owl
comes about old people we know
and the sky turns
and the bridge between daylight and night
stretches like a clothesline with our words.
Our surefootedness, one breath
through earth and sky—
our arms, braided roots.
We can sit down with tobacco,
lay our thoughts against the burning stars.

₪ Saved

…Bajo ese recuerdo, que te era quemadura,
caía la simiente de tu mano, serena.

Gabriela Mistral, "La mujer fuerte"

ON MONDAY EVENING, THE RADIATORS HOLD THEIR BREATH

She had been waiting for a touch like this—
the brushing thigh in a *bolero*—
Eve waiting on a bite of that first fruit.
And he comes already broken,
fingers leaking the cold light of the moon.
Pa-pi-to she had wanted to say...
And the clink and the clank,
cold ironwork of an age
announcing him
where rats squealed
into winter winds rising
to the thirteenth floor.
On the thirteenth floor
where the radiators stopped breathing
and Papo reached for Alice
with *bolero* thighs—*un bolero más, please*
—finding Alice or Eve
a little too sweet for pain.

WINDOW-SHOPPING

He couldn't afford a coat again this year,
wore every sweatshirt he owned.
Speeding past windows, Alice
took him from 7th Street.
Away the yuppie faces swarming Chinatown.
Winter's sweet when you got some soup
and no cold-stone blues
brewing in your beer,
Alice in the warmth of a thirteenth floor.
When Papo looks on her
the moon rises from her mouth
into the velvet evening—
makes him want to speak,
makes him want to stand up.

SAVED

She never met a man who
didn't like to do it
in the morning.
But Papo was best.

Away the rustle of cotton,
a slick probing in the ear,
to spring her hands to light.

She woke inside
wet mouth and shudder,
a blue lagoon
lapping over hip and flank.

All honey, *mont Vénus*
hailing the sap of the world.
Drink from this tree
and ye shall be saved.

Drink from this hallowed
earth and thy tribes shall come
from light, breaking.

OCTOBER OVER COLUMBIA ROAD

People crowd along, all shades of brown,
making way for vendors selling their pirated
CDs and oils in their tarp-roof shacks.
And the women in their *delantales*—
the crowd makes way for them too—heads
wrapped in scarves, selling *atól de elote*,
maybe a *pupusa*, or one of those green
mangoes you eat with *chile* till winter gets on.
I remember when all I wanted
was the streets like this—October bursting
from the trees, hot coffee with Gustavo
from Granada, talking politics. It was only yesterday
that I began to see Papo's hands
in the color of everything.

GRIOT

Saturday adrift
on the wings of a strange bird,
Spanish shrieking.

Blue smoke in the cold air
beneath helicopters.

He spins bodega loves
come and gone,
low-down addictions,
who got turned back.

He could graffiti a poem
back of the only bus here
if only it would come to him.

THIS MINUTE

If I ask myself
what I'd do about him,
I don't know. Bombs
are falling on people right
now. We're each alone.
Sometimes alone together.
Truth is, this alone shit
helps me breathe.
Trouble loves company, man.
I saw it in his eye.
Kissed it from him.

HELIOTROPE

A lover's door slammed in the face.
Rush-hour traffic of rats.
One-dimensional muck.
Two-dimensional gutter.
No verses held at the bodega.
Tony had laid his last.
Margarita, in for a beer,
rubbed one thigh against another
while she looked in on him.
Hands in pockets,
Papo stood post at the corner.
Even the windows around him
stared him down.
A cold wind now
rustled his sleeves and he could
breathe once more.
Take this breath, he said,
thinking of Alice, this one man's breath.

HORSES

No, I don't know shit about horses.
I only see them in some of the dogs
that walk through here.
See them in the bear I've seen at the zoo.
Dark is all these things that
remind me of horses.
Dark like the wind
against the street with its light bulb eyes.
Dark like you own the ground.
And your own running.
This is the year of my horses.
They leap from my skin,
let loose on the block.
Bare back.
This is the year.
I speak horse with my skin
and own the language
of hoofs hitting the ground.
My wind and my way out.
I came with horses into this dark
of no wind.
Prepared.
And unprepared.

CEREMONIES

You learn early
you have to make your own rituals.
You can sit with the Buddha
and do a thousand prostrations.
You can sweat till you drop
and dwell on the sage
singed against rocks.
You can dance and you can cheat
and brush your teeth screaming.
I've seen it in pigeons
and with gunk in my eyes
sitting on a bench in the park—
the woman inside *The Man
Who Had No Idea*—feeling
stupid seeing
how the world I breathe
was made with my stupid breath—
spit on a sidewalk,
a tree shedding its leaves.
How we need ritual.
Repeat. Repeat after me—
miracle me.
I can disappear, same time
every dusk come,
lay down on the floor
and still be one with the air.
I can long for Papo in the doing I do,
make him vanish when I have to.
My *bendición* and my *santigüo*.
The rock in my shoe.
Repeat. Repeat after me.

FRONT CHURCH STEPS

He talks about himself,
strict first-person worldview,
watches woman passing—
such a pity how everyone carries
a cell phone now,
not a second to look up,
spare a glance at calamity,
single out the faces.
It is unusually warm
for November
even though the sun is sinking,
barely a nose above water.
He hangs from his "I"—
resolute, pleading.

THE DOUBLE

Someone forgot to mention that she—
the other—pedaled
in suicidal dives toward ice,
and this face,
Guadalupe herself, fallen.

Someone forgot to point out
the birthplace of her sorrow—
impalpable things of the air,
Lavoe's dying croon.

From January's vacancy signs—
tattered above snow and shiver
—she appeared.
Love, masked in the nude
shoulder, the smoldering breast.

WINTER SOLSTICE

I watch his Kangol cap,
the damp night street.

I watch from the window
—with my tired feet,
my lost words.

Watch him
passed bright streetlamp,
vast shadow of brick
where he becomes shadow—

children's laughter,
old women's sorrow.

The moon keeps back.

In my dream crows fly there
and never come out
to live in two worlds.

I have blown my breath
into that shadow,
and seen bats nest in the eaves.
They send off
the sound of his footsteps.

I watch him leave—
mine—the cigarette in the mouth,
his dragging feet,
the streetlamp and the shadow.

From my throat,
the knocking of sugarcane
in the late afternoon.
From my feet, ferries glide off.

PARAMOUR

She woke from paralyzed
hands and feet to three a.m. scowls
behind the window—swollen,
wet from the ghostly kiss.

With ancient tongue
he'd traced her.

She was sure she'd give in
despite the way
her breath gave out
Tethered to him,
her nipples ready to find
any moist hole in the earth.

A Tewa once told her
about them—whelps,
incubus and succubus
some called fallen angels.
They woke fire.
Uninvited, made way and took.

She was sure she'd go.
Nights moored
like buoys in the sea.
And she, becoming fever
without bones
was leaving
where Papo could not go.

SAUDADE

I leave you now, my friend,
this perfect night.
Ursa Major above the hills,
the moon resting on the crowns
of Windham's pines.
I bless the day that brought you,
the coffee and the bread,
the knife that sliced the loaf.
I leave you fall
getting on in brown,
wood smoke in the crisp air.
I served your love.
Your love served me.

רֵ Perfection

Darkness,
You are forever.
Aho.
You are before the light.
Aho.
You are the smoke of the silence burning.
Aho.
Above, below, beyond,
among the glittering things, you are.

N. Scott Momaday, "Prayer"

After Taha Behbahani's painting "The Interior"
in *A Breeze from the Gardens of Persia:
New Art from Iran*, Getty Gallery, Los Angeles Public Library, 2002

INTERIORS

A woman dreams a dream,
not her life,
but often lives there.

The place of a wingless eagle,
a broad-swept curve
in a red-orange sky.

Stairwells,
like in stucco buildings
of California, Arizona,
rising up the neck
to the eagle's throat

into Her quiet shut mouth,
into Her quiet exact eye.

Only entrances,
so many musty and old,
like some dream entrances,
and no way out,

only the eagle's eye,
Her shut mouth.

Is this Iran?
The inside of a woman?

May we speak,
as women do,

of all our entrances,
our connected ways and means,
our missed flights?

We rise into freedom,
rise, rise as if
from the dead sometimes,
into our own interiors—

dreaming and waking,
sometimes
showing each other in secret
our secret wings,

weaving a story,
pretending to cook,
to tend, to aid.

PERFECTION

I bring back your drum and forgive you, body,
for cursing yourself
when you were accused
of endangering my salvation

and knelt to search for sin—
brewing shame like a back-home tea
out of woman-song.

I release you of sin,
the laws used to yoke you.

I release you from the colonialist's hymns—
aching back against the hardening
pews of your Sunday mornings,

when songbirds were put off
and you lost
the earth beneath your feet.

I forgive you the aches and fires
of your first moons—

you tried to wash them off like rape
with the same hands
you used to imitate the flight of birds,
to speak a poem.

MUKILTEO

for Jason

I don't remember much
about Mukilteo.
Perhaps the afternoon was clear
in the concrete streets.

After Tahoma,
after airport and too much coffee,
in the shuttle headed there,
two old people
huddled like birds.

Wisps of hair the color of smoke.
A pendent cheek
pressed against another.
She, ash and ember.
He, bones holding up the world.

They may have kissed.
His hand, a quivering leaf on her thigh.

The blind discomfort
of fused vertebrae had made
her shoulders a raven's.
His knuckles large from the weight
of lifting fences, rapped
gently on her arms.

After 50 years, she told me smiling,
two old people still lie beside each other
making and unmaking.

At the Mukilteo pier,
waiting on the Whidbey Island ferry,
a man offers me fried fish, and I eat
making my way around the lovers.

WALKING

I woke up a Bodhisattva
in the rain today—
meant to return to places
I have left screaming.
Trying to sing but not
really singing,

I spent hours in the woods
talking to a 10 year old who knew
much more about the world than I.

Everything has Buddha nature,
we remind each other,
even our sandals and our walking.

Compassion is a Buddha.
We will no doubt die
by our own hand—
so some people think,
the boy says.
Compassion will be responsible.

Maybe a spore of it,
the boy and I muse,
will take one of us as host, fruit
into a *corpse finder*,
if and when we're laid down to rest
here in this ground in *America*.

The last laugh
will be ours then, for those
who pass will make
our walking here longer still,
bearing our spores
to other cities,
other forests.

SUBJECTS

for the children of Sonoma State Hospital

Every war begins with taking.
And where the pursed
mouths of love released them,
white halls cut off their breath,

led them to stark sheets and uniformed
midwives of goggles,
cold metal and x-rays, the lines
their naked bodies formed.

I hear the wild grass scream,
the sun cut itself open.

Poisoned with fever and nightmare, they died
like a blue moon dies
at daybreak, like the beaten
on the city streets.

Forced libraries of medicine,
their kin's ethylene,
they were returned
incomplete and without names
to the ground, where wild
weeds regenerate
beneath the digger's hands.

Every war begins with those
who do not want to know
and leave—their hands shaking
before they let go.

With the tribute to the fallen came reminders
that the war against terror continues, that it is still
a time of color-coded warnings and constant threat.
Volunteers in Alexandria urged passersby to remain
vigilant as they distributed emergency preparedness kits.

—Christian Davenport and Carol Morello
Washington Post, Sunday, September 12, 2004

RED

In the eyes of children,
death's sandstorms.
Women cradle
pitted bellies.

An old man's shinbone
buried like a pole,
splits the bloody wind.

And here, today
a Red day—
color-code for alarm, a call
for everyone to turn
spy, sentry

to fear every face,
every darkness
we cannot name.

THIS SIDE OF EARLY

It's never too late here,
just this side of early.
The black bubblegum-starred sidewalk
a Milky Way twin where
the woman with a flower headwrap
squats to piss into expansion
and is hauled off by cops.
And sirens redden the tail of the universe
and pigeons swoop to peck on chicken bones,
all falling into the spiral,
into car horns with dreams.
Fluorocarbon winds dance their drunk dance,
rise and fall into the spiral.
Vendors salute and spit.
Market doors cough and inhale.
And lovers sell the moon down,
down into the sidewalk.
They hang their kisses from awnings,
hold down a corner, tag tomorrow.
Wanting to run and wanting to sit
we pant with lack, choke on specials—
this side of early, into expansion,
so old, we haven't been born yet.

Rookwood, July

Every day a new cocoon
and every night
a wing tip out.
The stars are bright
and do not care.
The city, with its loud,
hungry mouth, goes on.
I put my finger to the wind,
cast out a single
memory of flight.

AGAPANTHUS RHIZOME

Tossed it in my garden
that it might fight weeds
and I not hear it craving water.
Upstairs in the house,
covered my ears and crossed my legs,
shut the blinds,
put on loud music.

It knew rains would come,
rooted and divided,
beat against the window panes,
traveled on the tongues and feet of bees.
I thought to cut it down
but the phone kept ringing
and I was hungry.

Frost came early and the ground
was laced with blooms.
So deep blue still,
I placed some in glass bowls,
pinned a handful to my blouse.

NAMING

for Lyll

The little beast kicked inside,
tilting her toward the floor.
She balanced whole
and prayed for water.

Today it was a retching monkey,
a giant mantis, a bullock at Pamplona's run.
Last night, a thing out
of another universe, un-twin,
choking, begging for food.

She—of the sea and to a sea
returning—
named it a thousand things,
tried not to curse it.

Well, *Wave* then. *Saudade.*
Sky in Spring.
Laughter from a Long-Gone Day.
Nana's Song.
Life came pushing
and making room,
every-day ugly and beautiful.

GASOLINE

She had narrow hands,
long slim fingers she liked to place
along her jaw.

One split soul,
we walked side by side
along the countryside
for hours, without a word.

She was poorer
than I was poor.

Her house,
farther down the hill,
was nearly always empty.
I was never allowed in it.
She was never
allowed in mine.

She wore a wrap sometimes
to flatten the front of her hair
against her scalp, the back
always like a mound at dusk,
making evening beautiful.

The day I followed her
to the latrine she thanked me,
averted her eyes,
set the plastic jug
beside my legs,
told me what to do.

Bent over the hole,
her head of Spanish moss
drained the clear liquid.
It was the only way,

her mother had told her,
to kill the lice—

her mother I had never seen,
a mother Betty whispered about
as though her ears
were the very earth,
her mother who loved her
more than I.

We were each
nearly eleven then,
never worried
about the next day,
never longed for the future.

IN THE BENNINGTON WOOD

The sky's been shedding
two days straight.

Every word from me
a brittle, iced over bough

pulled from memory—
against me and yet on my behalf.

Here the wood ends,
where my blood

pools in my thighs
in search of its ocean.

The wood is empty.
The wind pulls in a crow

to watch over finding
the last of my moons.

Twelve Days

i.

No amniotic whisper
would carry the news
of first blood or last.

ii.

She wept over me, a swollen belly
month in and out
until at the hospital
abuela took me from her
so she could breathe.
She never woke from crying.

iii.

A man tells me
I am the bearer of nations,
Woman.
And I laugh
beside the camp fire,
trying to bear a different fruit
while feeding the hungry,
aiding the ailing
with new languages.

iv.

Forced to wash my own blood
in a public sink
same breath I'm told
I'll bleed many moons.

What do women *do*
who faint at the sight of this?

How do they learn
to be with their bodies?

We were buying my brother a raft.
I was allowed to swim only
this one time,
wet my hair this once.
Later, locked in my room.
¡El gallo cantó!
¡El gallo cantó!
The rooster has sung
for me whose blood comes,
this woman.

v.

This is not a love poem
but I have loved her.
I was her blood
before I was half of everything.

vi.

They came
bearing the gifts of their biology
finding mine a little too
brown,
a little
too red,
a little too dirty sometimes.
Are you *marked*?
Are you *shifting*?
Where is your body's tattoo?

vii.

Others blessed the simple renewal
joined one bank to the other

with a bridge of wet stones.
Blood of my blood.
Blood of my people.

viii.

I watch her go from me,
my moon,
my gravity.

ix.

Tonight I wake fighting the sheets
as if bound,
while still alive,

in the wet cloths
that would preserve me.

x.

Deep tracks in the Vermont snow.
I conjure crones,
ask this about my breasts,
this about my fevers,
the earth's thunder rising up my feet.

xi.

The last of this blood
is the last of my mother in me.
And she will never be here
to sing.

xii.

Love lives outside my body,
love in root.

Water, fire
beyond the moon,
the icy boughs.

BURROWING

Two-foot tree with lights
crowned with a red ribbon,
bearing your beaded dragonfly.

Why am I like this
when lights shine
and you are in my way like a tear?

I squat near the radiator
and the window.
Not so many rats out.
Not a broken bottle,
a dog squeal,
a man, nauseated,
bending over the tolerant curb.

And it's not three a.m.
and I'm smoking a cigarette.

Once I was a girl
under a Christmas tree
towering above me like a sequoia—
pretty because little colored lights
make a girl feel pretty

and trees make you
mind your size.

I was only a girl
for a short while.

I'd meet my secret shames,
find a hidden spot to cry,
let the weight come down.

I remember my hands,

burrowing in the night
without hands.

Tonight I watch
your keepsake dragonfly,
waiting for snow to bear down
on the branches of token trees
in the prisons of their boxes.

ENGAGEMENT

Suburban mall
of Trumbull, Connecticut.
He buys this Hopi ring
in the touring sales exhibit—
four turquoise tear drops,
one full abalone moon.
In the thick heat
the sale signs hail their prices.
I take the ring in my hand
before he slips it
on my finger, know tonight
the Juniper leaves
behind the house will turn
away. My nana moon
will laugh. The sitting
stones will be cold and empty.
One promise about to be half-made,
another fully broken.

THE FATE OF THE ROSES

This apology in red
dies in the wild
among forgotten kin
who welcome
perfected beauty
for the food it is.
The fire ants
bear the lightness
of let-go petals,
feast of worms,
new home of aphids.
Regrets, like raindrops
the night might feed on.

VISIT

In my dream he fed me moth wings
and I woke
wearing my finest tee
—15 years worn-thin.

Arriving home in work clothes
the night before,
he leaned my body
against the pantry door,
removed each piece of clothing
like marks that insult the body,
felt me up a half hour or more.
I creamed my soul.

It has always been like this.
I don't have to ask
too many questions.
He comes and he goes.

I'm five miracles away
from true happiness.
I've already learned to cry.

BODHISATTVA

The Bodhisattva emerges
from the foot of the mountain,
a brown-eyed Korean
in a wool cap.
He makes teaberry leaf
tea with mint, mullein,
Juniper berries.
The earth lives under his fingers.
He sees the world through the eyes
of fungi jellies, slimes,
polypores.
I almost did not speak
to him the first time.
For many days now
we've been telling time
by the singing of a mockingbird,
have built fires, prayed together.
I leave him now
for who knows how long
and have not yet watched his feet
move along the mountains.
They must grip the earth
like mycelium,
their love of soil and wood spread
one hundred infinite yards or more,
remembering like an *Earthstar*
the way home.

SUMMER SOLSTICE

Autumn arrives inside of June,
daylight dying on the mountains.
And the tall grasses bend
in the wind.

I fill up the world's empty spaces—
a man's voice I do not know
calls me near,
the geography of my mother's kitchen,
my father's hand waving.

I'm tired of streets and wheels
and the urban howl of anyone's misfortune.
I come through this yellow day
with the clothes on my back,
with my ancient eyes and sallow shadow.

I could cross the wood now
and climb the ridges, aged
and aging, tired of being of use.

ONE

What do I know about anything?
The rain comes down.
I am lonely like a tattered hat.
Who would say
there are stars in my shoes?
Words of lightning?
My body's full of life's sticks.
Alive and gurgling,
doubt sucks at my left breast.
A plane cuts across the sky
every other hour now that it is night.
So low, it is in my chest.
There in the sky and here in my chest—
like my heart. Far away,
I yearn toward my center,
as I yearn inside it—
not two ways of being, but one.

CRICKETS

I don't know where crickets go
when the frost comes.
Do they freeze on the spot?
Make their way to farmhouses, barns?
Do they burrow? Make tiny homes
between bricks and concrete cracks?
I don't want to know.
It's better like this.
Their song quiets me
when I'm alone near the dark,
dark side of the woods,
when I sit to long
for things I can't bear to name.
I think I want to be a cricket when I die—
singing among thousands,
punctuating the air with song
for those who visit with the night.
I want to go where it is I go
and come back singing, always, somehow.

NOTES

You in the Me of I

"Hole," page 3
- *abuelo* – grandfather

"Every Throat," page 4
- *coquí* – small tree-frog native to Puerto Rico and national symbol of the island; named after the sound of its singing
- *tabaqueras* – women who worked the tobacco fields, who both picked and dried tobacco leaves; sometimes used to mean *despalilladoras*, those whose task it was to remove the stems of the tobacco leaves with their teeth
- *abuelo* – grandfather

"Cutter," page 5
- *mosquitero* – mosquito net that is tied to bed posts
- *dubi-du* – a way to style hair by rolling the strands in the crown onto a giant roller (or, as used traditionally, a tin can opened at both ends), and wrapping the remaining hair flat against and around the scalp with bobby pins in order to straighten coarse hair or add waves to long straight hair
- *maleza* – underbrush, scrub

"*Cada Vez*," page 8
- *cada vez* – every time
- *Cada vez que los nombro, resucitan mis muertos* – Every time I name them my dead are resurrected
- *papi* – daddy (in this usage)

"*Barro*," page 11
- *barro* – clay
- *Cagüana* – deity of the Taíno (indigenous people of Puerto Rico) associated with fertility; the reference to squatting over hot stones refers to the belief that pregnant Taíno women would do so to help them dilate when they neared the time of birthing
- *maíz* – Taíno word for corn

- hurakán – Hurakán was a Taíno deity; also the indigenous word for hurricane

"Jesus Comes to Mt. Pleasant in Search of Sanzen," page 16
- Sanzen – in many traditions of Zen, a formal interview with a teacher
- koan – a Zen teaching riddle meant to temporarily jam normal cognitive processing

Saved

Opening epigram
- From the poem "The Strong Woman," *Bajo ese recuerdo, que te era quemadura, caía la simiente de tu mano, serena* – Beneath that memory, that was a burn to you, fell the seed of your hand, serenely

"On Monday Evening the Radiators Hold their Breath," page 21
- *bolero* – slow dance

"October Over Columbia," page 24
- *delantales* – aprons (whether short and tied at the waist, or full and hanging from the neck, usually homemade of colorful print fabrics with lace ribbons bordering the edges)
- *atól de elote* – a sweet corn drink (typically from El Salvador and Mexico), served hot for breakfast
- *pupusa* – an *empanada*-like finger food from El Salvador, made from white corn flour and Salvadoran cheese (sometimes stuffed with beef or chicken), served with carrot sauce and shredded cabbage

"Ceremonies," page 29
- *bendición* – blessing
- *santigüo* – in Puerto Rico, the ritual of rubbing the belly with olive oil while making a prayer to ease stomach ache and other types of malaise
- *The Man Who Had No Idea* – title of a science fiction short story by Thomas Disch: In a new society, people

must have a license to speak and in order to secure it, one must pass an exam that requires one to have and present an *original* idea; we follow the protagonist on a long, frustrating journey where every original idea has already been taken, till he stumbles upon one while observing the comings and goings of pigeons

"The Double," page 31

- Epigram – *The myth of the doppelgänger postulates that every human being has, somewhere in the world, a double of himself.* The article (10 September 2000) goes on to say: *Its appearance is identical, like that of a twin, but its character is always the opposite of its double. Meeting one's double face to face is usually interpreted as an omen of death.*
- *Guadalupe* – as in *La Virgen de Guadalupe*; the brown Virgin Mary of the people of Central and South America
- *Lavoe* – as in Héctor Lavoe, renowned 70s salsa singer of the Fania All-Stars

"Saudade," page 34

- *saudade* – from the Portuguese; homesickness; sorrow

Perfection

"Walking," page 41

- *Bodhisattva* – Buddhist deity; symbol of compassion; Bodhisattva's vow is to forego the gift of her own enlightenment till she has ascertained that each creature has first attained it
- *Corpse finder* (*Hebeloma syriense*) – a type of mushroom common to the northeast of the United States (thought by some to grow only in North America); used in some forensic investigations, the *corpse finder* grows only where corpses are buried; one theory holds that, while alive, humans pick up and carry its spores

"Subjects," page 42

- *Sonoma State Hospital* – created in 1885 in Santa Clara, CA and originally named The California Home for the

Care and Training of Feeble-Minded Children; the new facility, located near Glen Ellen, was opened in 1891; the name was changed to Sonoma State Home in 1915. Now known as the Sonoma Developmental Center and the site where children and adults with developmental disabilities were used in medical and scientific studies (most renowned, in radiation experiments) without permission from their families; similar studies are credited with leading to the development of the polio and hepatitis vaccine. Over 1,400 patients are estimated to have been buried in the grounds outside the hospital, in an unmarked field, and the cremated remains of others kept in a local vault; further, the brain of every patient with cerebral palsy was removed post-mortem and kept for study by the facility

"Agapanthus Rhizome," page 46

- *Agapanthus* - comes from the Greek *agape* (love) and *anthos* (flower); Agapanthus, also known as African Lilies and Lilies-of-the-Nile, produce clumps of long, shiny, strap-like leaves; stems reach 2 to 6 feet in height, and are topped with clusters of white to dark blue flowers from late spring to early autumn
- *rhizome* - horizontal, usually underground stem of a plant that often sends out roots and shoots from its nodes; it is thought that Karl Jung was one of the firsts to use the word: *Life has always seemed to me like a plant that lives on its rhizome. Its true life is invisible, hidden in the rhizome. The part that appears above the ground lasts only a single summer. Then it withers away - an ephemeral apparition. When we think of the unending growth and decay of life and civilizations, we cannot escape the impression of absolute nullity. Yet I have never lost the sense of something that lives and endures beneath the eternal flux. What we see is blossom, which passes. The rhizome remains.* (Prologue from *Memories, Dreams, Reflections*)

"Twelve Days," page 51

- *abuela* – grandmother
- *El gallo cantó* – literally, *the rooster has sung*; a reference to an old Puerto Rican practice where mothers

confined their daughters to a room for the duration of menarche; the practice began with the mother, or parents, announcing the events by shouting the words to friends and relatives

"Bodhisattva," page 60

- *Earthstar* – a fungus of the Geaster genus; its outer coating splits into the shape of a star, and the inner one forms a ball containing dust-like spores

CURBSTONE PRESS, INC.

is a nonprofit publishing house dedicated to multicultural literature that reflects a commitment to social awareness and change, with an emphasis on contemporary writing from Latino, Latin American, and Vietnamese cultures.

Curbstone's mission focuses on publishing creative writers whose work promotes human rights and intercultural understanding, and on bringing these writers and the issues they illuminate into the community. Curbstone builds bridges between its writers and the public—from inner-city to rural areas, colleges to cultural centers, children to adults, with a particular interest in underfunded public schools. This involves enriching school curricula, reaching out to underserved audiences by donating books and conducting readings and educational programs, and promoting discussion in the media. It is only through these combined efforts that literature can truly make a difference.

Curbstone Press, like all non-profit presses, relies heavily on the support of individuals, foundations, and government agencies to bring you, the reader, works of literary merit and social significance that would likely not find a place in profit-driven publishing channels, and to bring these authors and their books into communities across the country.

If you wish to become a supporter of a specific book—one that is already published or one that is about to be published—your contribution will support not only the book's publication but also its continuation through reprints.

We invite you to support Curbstone's efforts to present the diverse voices and views that make our culture richer, and to bring these writers into schools and public places across the country. Tax-deductible donations can be made to:
Curbstone Press, 321 Jackson Street, Willimantic, CT 06226
phone: (860) 423-5110 fax: (860) 423-9242
www.curbstone.org